DEMOCRA
SCIENCE, AND
THE CIVIC SPIRIT

An Inaugural Lecture
delivered before
the University of Oxford
on 27 October 1992

by

STEIN RINGEN

Professor of Sociology
and Social Policy

CLARENDON PRESS · OXFORD
1993

Oxford University Press, Walton Street, Oxford OX2 6DP

Oxford New York Toronto
Delhi Bombay Calcutta Madras Karachi
Kuala Lumpur Singapore Hong Kong Tokyo
Nairobi Dar es Salaam Cape Town
Melbourne Auckland Madrid

and associated companies in
Berlin Ibadan

Oxford is a trade mark of Oxford University Press

Published in the United States by
Oxford University Press Inc., New York

British Library Cataloguing in Publication Data
Data available

Library of Congress Cataloging in Publication Data
Ringen, Stein.
Democracy, science, and the civic spirit : an inaugural lecture /
delivered before the University of Oxford on 27 October 1992 by
Stein Ringen.
1. Democracy. 2. Civics. 3. Science and civilization.
I. Title.
JC423.R515   1993
321.8—dc20   93-18200
ISBN 0-19-951359-7

Typeset and printed in
Great Britain by Oxuniprint
Oxford University Press
Walton Street, Oxford

DEMOCRACY, SCIENCE, AND THE CIVIC SPIRIT

AT the end of 1989 and the beginning of 1990 I found myself in Chile, right after the successful congressional elections and during the days when the Chileans were finally able to feel confident that democracy would be restored. We who have grown up in Western Europe after the Second World War have never experienced the loss of freedom. That is our good fortune, of course, but we should also be aware that we do not *know* the physical reality of oppression. This was brought home to me during a long evening in the company of a dignified Chilean, an elderly lady whose husband had disappeared during the dictatorship, whose son had been killed by having his throat cut in broad daylight in central Santiago, and whose daughter had been in exile until the year before, and who was now herself elected *Diputada* for the *Partido por la Democracia*, one of the parties in the *Concertación* which beat the Pinochet crowd in the elections. As she told her story, in a soft-spoken way which was unreal to me, this visiting North European learned something about democracy, and in particular the danger of its absence.

In my book *The Possibility of Politics*, I tried to analyse the welfare state in such a way as to comment on the feasibility of piecemeal, step-by-step, reformist policies. In intellectual circles, reform is suspect as seen from both left and right. I was therefore delighted, being a middle-of-the-road man myself, to be able to pass a favourable verdict on the power of reform.

I have always associated political reform with political democracy. I believe that democracy generates reform because it will not be accepted to let problems lie where they fall. I also believe that democracy limits politics to reform since majorities will accept

I am grateful to Bjørn Hvinden, Natalie Rogoff Ramsøy, Anders Ringen, Mariken Vaa, and Gerd Vandeskog, who heard an early version and suggested many improvements, and to Susan Dyson for innumerable rounds of re-editing.

revolutions to democracy but not revolutionary shifts within democracy. In a sense, therefore, the analysis I was conducting was about reason in the muddled arrangements of the mixed-economy democracy. I did not feel, however, that I could extend the analysis at that time to the issue of democracy. 'If it were not,' I wrote in an introductory section, 'that I already have more than a reasonable share of broad questions on my plate I might have been tempted to add, Is democracy possible?'

I resisted the temptation then, wisely I'm sure. Today, however, I intend to give in and to take up the question I then felt I had to set aside. After all, this is an occasion on which it is accepted—perhaps even encouraged—to address issues which would in other circumstances be frivolous. So, then, does democracy work?

I have a professional interest in the application of social science to issues of concern in society. Applied research is intended to contribute to something practical. What social research contributes to is perhaps not always clear. I want to argue that we have a role to play in the workings of democracy and that a programme for applied social science can be formulated in terms of fulfilling this role.

The last few years have seen revolutions of democracy throughout the world. I have in mind, obviously, Eastern Europe, but also the Philippines, Argentina, Zambia, South Africa (hopefully), Nicaragua, and certainly Chile—once the democratic pride of South America, then the world's most despised dictatorship, and now again a working democracy. I think of the fall from grace of the outlandish idea in Africa that one-party rule is necessary because of African tradition. I have in mind the eradication (almost) of military rule in Latin America and the many attempts, although some unsuccessful so far, in the direction of democracy in, for example, China, Nigeria, Burma, Bangladesh, Kenya, Côte d'Ivoire, Algeria, and not least the tragedy of Haiti, where the first free elections after almost 200 years of independence were soon enough set aside. Having visited that country several times and become captured by the cultural richness of a proud people suffering no end of political corruption and material deprivation—this is a land where the very physical soil has been plundered—I feel that I have experienced the degradation and destructiveness of bad government in its extreme form, and I assure you it stimulates thought about good government. Those who need to see for themselves the price of non-democracy in the elementary life chances of ordinary people, let them go to Haiti.

The logic of applied research is that the researcher puts to use his or her tool-box for resolving some problem which arises from the conduct of practical affairs. There are odd problems which serious scholars would not be bothered with and there are wicked problems which scholars of integrity would not touch, but generally, in applied research, we take on problems such as they are presented to us.

In the social sciences, problems are often presented to us by 'decision-makers'. That is as it should be, but as a programme it is too narrow. The act of decision-making, certainly in a democracy, is only the final step in a long process which leads up to the moment of truth when it is decided to do A and not to do B. A proper ambition for the social sciences is to respond to the whole range of problems which arise in this entire process and not only to those of the final stage. The clients of applied social research are not only decision-makers, but rather, and primarily, the public—the women and men who participate in politics as citizens. We should take up not only those problems which are articulated by decision-makers but any problems which present themselves from the process itself, however they may or may not be articulated. We should work for the political process rather than for the politicians.

The democratic revolution is enormously positive, but also chilling. The most troubled peoples of the world are turning to democracy for solutions to their problems. I am quite convinced that they are right in so doing, but the burden the democratic system of government is now asked to carry is staggering. More is expected than can be delivered. The coming of democracy to the former Soviet Union is not exactly celebrated as a triumph. In

Czechoslovakia, the Velvet Revolution tore the Federation apart. In the first free elections in Poland last year, and likewise in Zambia, only about 40 per cent of the electorate chose to use the right to vote which they had just won.

In the established democracies we may feel safe, but I suggest we should not be complacent. It has happened before that democracy is lost. We cannot take it for granted that our democracies are strong enough to stand if the democratic experiments around us fail. On the European scene, some politicians seem to believe in super-national power without democratic institutions. 'Democracies have always been, and still are, failure prone. They were short lived, and by all accounts ill suited for survival . . .' Thus we are reminded by Giovanni Sartori of the historical experience. Horrors we thought were confined to the scrap-heap of history in our part of the world, are in these days proving themselves to be alive and well. We need at this time to be deadly serious about the importance and difficulty of democracy and to give careful thought to its meaning and practical mechanics.

Democracy

As soon as people live in society, there will be a need for collective decisions on things which have to be done communally and on norms for co-operation. This is true of small societies, such as families, and it is true of large societies, such as those we call nations— and for that matter of the global society.

In large societies we use the term *politics* to denote the system for making and implementing collective decisions. Democratic systems have one thing in common with all other political systems and are in one respect different from all alternatives. What all political systems have in common is that they are mechanisms for producing decisions. What distinguishes democracies from other political systems is the way in which decisions are produced.

Both aspects are important. We often, and rightly, judge

democracies by their specific quality, how decisions are made. But we also need to consider them in terms of what they have in common with other systems, their ability to produce decisions. Democracy is not just a way of sharing responsibility, it is also an arrangement for getting on with the job.

Let me try to explain further through some simple and rather formalistic observations. I split the larger process in two, first the process in which collective decisions are made, and then the process through which they are implemented. Both these processes can be understood as movements, so to speak, back and forth between the individual and collective levels in society. In the first instance, individual preferences aggregate into a collective will, as when citizens cast votes in a referendum. In dictatorships this is simple because the preferences of a single person, or a small clique, are imposed as the collective will. In a democracy it is complicated because the collective will has to be forged out of a large number of individual preferences, all of which ideally count equally, and many of which will be in discord.

In the second round, the collective will disaggregates into individual actions to carry it out. The simple example is taxation. We decide collectively on a certain level and distribution of taxes and this decision is carried out when each of us pays the tax which is expected. The collective will is usually followed by various forms of encouragement and control to comply, but in the final analysis it comes down to the individual. Parliaments and governments can only make two kinds of decisions, about rules of conduct and about the spending of money. Such decisions will come to naught unless citizens adapt their behaviour to the collective expectation. No amount of government spending on health services could have any effect whatsoever if innumerable doctors, nurses, technicians, and administrators were not willing to carry to the patients the services which the spending is intended to buy.

In the process of making collective decisions, democracies give each citizen the same say. This is the democratic ideal, pure and simple. It is a simple ideal to express but strong assumptions are required in order to see how it could become reality. The most important of these assumptions are, first, that all citizens are well and equally informed, secondly, that they have the same opportunity and ability to make their voices heard, and thirdly, that the decision-making process is without distortions which amplify some voices and mute others.

As strong as these assumptions are, they are not utopian. They are the rules we apply to voting: one person one vote, free access to the ballot, and meticulous care in the counting of votes so that all votes are counted and each only once. Through political campaigns, we go to great lengths to inform voters about their options, and we accept that everyone is sufficiently informed to make a responsible choice (except that we persist in denying children the right to vote). Very considerable effort, organization, and expense is invested to protect the integrity of the vote. However, collective decision-making is not limited to the few occasions on which we vote, but occurs every day, in economic as well as political life. In all other situations than voting, we are not remotely near giving everyone the possibility, never mind the same possibility, for making their voices heard. There are differences in access to education, eloquence, connections, money, and—the top price—the 30-seconds slot in the evening news on television. The decision-making process is contaminated with no end of tricks to make some voices sound larger than life, in the form of organized interests, political action committees, and bishops pushing particular points of view from behind purple dog-collared shirts. Beyond the formal elegance of the vote, the democratic record of even the best of democracies is dismal.

In the process of implementation we should expect decisions democratically made to be accepted and complied with by all. Since everyone has had the same say, each decision reflects the best possible compromise. Our disagreements we bring to bear in the process of reaching collective decisions, and we can then fight like lions. Once the battle is over and a decision has been reached, we agree to accept the verdict because the fight has been fair, and we move our disagreements on to new issues which are not yet resolved. 'In a democracy,' explained Max Weber in an exchange with General Ludendorf, 'people choose a leader in whom they trust. Then the chosen leader says, "Now shut up and obey me." Later the people can sit in judgement. If the leader has made mistakes—to the gallows with him!'

To a remarkable degree we do accept what is expected of us. We drive on the same side of the road, we go to work, we do not beat our children. But non-compliance is still a problem, so much so that vast, unpleasant, and wasteful bureaucracies are needed for the purpose of control. It may not take elaborate controls to keep drivers on the same side of the road, but it does to impose speed limits, not to mention bringing in taxes. The reason is obvious. Collective decisions are compromises between conflicting interests. It will always be advantageous for some to avoid the consequences. To ask for compliance is to ask some people to act contrary to their own benefit.

The two processes of democracy are closely linked. If we want compliance, we must make sure that decisions are made fairly. How can we ask people to comply if what they are asked to comply with reflects special interests rather than the general will? If we want fairness in decision-making, we must assure compliance. How can we ask people to participate in decision-making if what is decided is treated with indifference? However, although there is much interdependence in this system, it does not propel itself to perfection. Compliance and fairness are each other's necessary but not sufficient conditions. For democracy to work, citizens must want to make it work, and they must want that rather desperately.

Some general points follow from this discussion. First, the importance of the vote. This institution is important because when we use the vote, we do in fact all have the same say, and it is important because it symbolizes the reality on earth, if I may so say, of the heavenly ideal. The low voting participation in many elections is a sorry sign for democracy. Social scientists sometimes do not have much patience with formal procedures, but instead want to understand the realities behind the formalities, so much so that formalities may be ignored. Democracy is a complicated system, but its core is the elementary simplicity of the universal vote.

Second, the importance of equality. Democracy is based on equality, be it in the distribution of resources which influence decisions or the distribution of resulting benefits and burdens. 'The assumption,' writes Robert Dahl, 'that a rough equality in the distribution of resources facilitates a rough equality in the distribution of power or control over government is common in political theory since the classical Greek era.' Tocqueville, in *De la démocratie en Amerique*, found a high degree of social and economic equality to be necessary for democracy. Powerful egalitarian arguments have been advanced in the philosophical literature, for example by Tawney, based on the moral principle of the equal worth of all persons, or by Rawls in the logical experiment of the 'veil of ignorance' which suggests that opposition to equality is necessarily based on vested interests. Still, the old observation that democracy does not work unless everyone is included is perhaps the strongest of all arguments for the principle of equality.

Third, the importance of the individual citizen. Democracy is a big system, but it is not a mass phenomenon in which individuals disappear. Citizens depend on democracy for their freedom and democracy depends on the participation of citizens. There will be no democracy unless citizens vote and in other ways take part in the struggle over decisions. Nor will there be democracy unless citizens accept and carry out the decisions which are made. Democracy is not possible unless citizens want it, and it is not possible unless citizens behave democratically.

Science

In 1936 Ragnar Frisch, the pioneer in the theory of planning, who was, with Jan Tinbergen, to be the first Nobel Prize winner in economics, wrote a small memorandum which he entitled *Den prin-*

sipielle sondring mellom sak og vurdering. There is a richness of nuance in this Norwegian title which it is difficult to capture in English, so when I offer *The theoretical distinction between fact and value* as an English translation I am not doing full justice to the original.

Professor Frisch was concerned with the relationship between science and politics and with what social science could do for politics. He proceeded to define this relationship around the distinction between fact and value. Values enter science, he found, through the assumptions upon which analysis rests. Value problems can and should be resolved in assumptions. The remaining problems are then factual, and scientific analysis proper can start. Once assumptions are given, it is possible, although difficult, to achieve objectivity of analysis in the sense that results properly derived must be accepted by all who are competent to understand the research.

The politician also, still following Frisch, confronts both types of problems. The choice of goals is a value problem, as is the decision about which means are legitimate. Once this is established, however, the choice of means among those which are allowed is a problem of optimality which can be resolved through analysis.

From this Frisch went on to suggest what amounted to a division of labour between politics and science. Politicians should take care of the value element, they should set goals and establish the boundaries for what can and what cannot be done. The experts should then step in, take the value premises handed to them by the politicians as their assumptions, and find the most effective means.

Frisch stuck to this model throughout his life and never lost his confidence in the ability of science to find the right means once goals were given. But he became increasingly impatient with the politicians, who never seemed able to do their part of the job. In his despair he constructed an elaborate questionnaire which he intended to administer to the members of *Stortinget,* the Norwegian parliament, and through which he would force them to choose a consistent set of goals so that he and his colleagues could get to work on their computers and find the best means. This project never came to fruition, and no doubt that was just as well.

Any social science student of my generation who suffered years of agony at university under the wretched 'positivism debate' will shy away from Frisch's distinction between fact and value, but that is a trivial matter which there is no need to brood over here. Frisch wrote his memorandum when he was asked by a group of leading men in the business community to direct an ambitious study of 'economic structures'. There had been an element of expert rule thinking in the deliberations in this group and perhaps a suggestion that the economic conditions of the nation might have been better had expertise been trusted more and politics less. Such ideas were hardly surprising given the impotence of political authorities at the time to face up to the overwhelming problems of stagnation and unemployment, but any hint of super-political authority was, of course, extremely sensitive in Europe in the mid-1930s. Frisch was a radical in politics and he felt a need to formulate a position in which he disassociated himself from any suggestion of expert rule. Through our eyes it might seem that he handed over half of the political process to the experts, but, in the context of the time, what he did was to defend the primacy of politics over expertise.

As all first-year students know, the strict distinction between fact and value is not philosophically tenable, and the idea that the value problem in the social sciences can be cleared away by being confined to assumptions had been rejected at the time Frisch wrote his memorandum, notably by his colleague in Sweden, Gunnar Myrdal, in a dissertation published in 1929 (and republished in revised form in English in 1953 under the title *The Political Element in the Development of Economic Theory*). Those who want to rubbish my hero on this point will have a field day, but they will, I think, miss the essential. By suggesting a division of labour between politics and science, Frisch claimed not only that there are certain problems which only science can solve and for which scientists should take responsibility, but also that there are problems which science cannot solve and which scientists should therefore not take on. Exactly where to draw the line of demarcation may be in dispute, but that there is a line was right then and remains right today.

All forms of political decisions are political, be it the choice of goals or the use of means. No line of demarcation there. There is, nevertheless, a factual element in politics which is, in principle, non-political and upon which rational political action depends. This element is *information*. For citizens to participate in politics, they must be informed. Before political decisions can be made, there must be information on which to act. Having abandoned the line of demarcation between fact and value, I suggest an alternative line drawn between information and decision; between, on the one hand, the questions of how things *are* and what *can* be done, and, on the other hand, the question of what *should* be done. Let me, further, push to the background the politician and pull to the foreground the political process. Let me suggest information as the common ground between politics and science; information is what politics needs and science can provide. And let me, on this basis, and otherwise in Frisch's spirit of a division of labour, try to redefine the role of the social sciences in relation to the democratic process.

First, as social scientists we should accept responsibility for informing the democratic process. We should accept this responsibility (although shared with, for example, journalists and educators) because we are the custodians of the methodology which is best suited for the job of establishing how things are and what can be done. As has been pointed out by Sten Johansson, the political methods of discourse, struggle, conflict, and compromise are useless for resolving questions such as, Is public health improving or deteriorating? Are crime, violence, and child-abuse on the increase? What are the effects of changes in social security legislation on poverty? How widespread is the problem of stress in the work-place? Do tax cuts stimulate effort and initiative? No debate, however sophisticated, can produce reliable answers to questions such as these. These are empirical problems and empirical problems should be resolved by analysis. To great benefit for en-lightened politics, we do have generally accepted ways of answer-ing some persistent questions of this kind, for example about unemployment and inflation, but we need authoritative informa-tion on a much wider range of social and economic trends.

I want it to be added that there should be no delusion about the limits of analysis for producing irrefutable answers to empirical questions. The answers we produce will always be wrought with uncertainty and there will always be more questions asked than answers given. What I believe we can and should say, however, is that there is no alternative method to that of careful analysis which can do the job better. Had we wanted, in 1957, when Harold Macmillan told the British people, 'You've never had it so good', to ascertain whether he was right, we should not have organized a round table, we should have consulted the statistics or started a research project.

Second, we should not only accept responsibility for informing the political process, we should claim this as our authority. The political struggle does not stop at the domain of information. The concern of the politician is, rightly, to be elected or re-elected, to win power or to stay in power. Politicians who can doctor the data to their advantage will do so, and it is in the nature of competitive politics to spread disinformation. Since we cannot outlaw such be-haviour without outlawing democracy—indeed, since strong democracy depends on ruthlessly aggressive politics—there is a need to ensure that the political process is independently in-formed. Decisions taken from distortions will be the wrong deci-sions, but, much more importantly, citizenry control over politics is not possible without informed citizens. Hence, I do not agree with the great Henrik Ibsen who, when challenged, in a poem in 1875, wrote, 'I prefer to ask, it is not my calling to answer.' Our calling is, precisely, to answer.

In Britain today, government agencies retain ultimate control over the publication of research results from projects they have contracted. In the social sciences we are dependent on government contracts and we therefore do not have freedom to publish our results. This is a miserable state of affairs which should be brought to an end. It should be for the scientific community to decide, through its system of peer review, what and how to publish, and the power of the purse should make no difference to this. Contract research for government agencies is on behalf of the public and the public should know what the research finds. It does not matter that difficulties over publication usually do not arise, because it matters very much in the few cases when difficulties do arise—and there is always the possibility of self-censorship.

Third, although we should claim the domain of information as ours, we should, as social scientists, not transgress into the domain of decisions. As citizens we have the same rights as other citizens, but as scientists we have no special rights. We have some expertise with regard to how things are and work, and therefore responsibility to serve, but we have no competence on questions of what should be done, and therefore no special right to influence. If we use our expertise to inform the political process, we strengthen democracy on one of its central assumptions, that of an informed citizenry. If we claim authority which we do not have in order to gain influence, we weaken democracy on one of its other assumptions, that of a decision-making process without distortions. It is easy to be critical of others who use unfair means to win influence—for example, money. We need to be equally critical of our own ways. The academic community is not a nobility with special privileges. We should be activists, certainly, and when necessary prepared to confront politicians in the most forceful manner, but activists on the basis of legitimate authority. As social scientists we have no other expertise than information to offer; we cannot do surgery, we cannot build bridges, we cannot explode bombs. Personally, I feel that the job of information is important and sufficient, but even if I did not, I should be made to understand that I have no business trying to convince the world that I am an expert in the rights and wrongs of political decisions. Hence, I do not agree with the great Karl Marx who, in his *Theses on Feuerbach* in

1845 said, 'The philosophers have only *interpreted* the world; the point, however, is to *change* it.' Our job is, precisely, to interpret the world, and, precisely not, to change it.

The civic spirit

Above I have sketched the outlines of perfect democracy: informed citizens participating on equal terms and accepting the outcome of fair compromise. Could we make democracy work perfectly? The answer is that we could not, and, further, that we should not so much as think the thought.

Perfect democracy is an illusion, as is the idea of perfection generally. There will never be equality in the distribution of means of influence. Even if equality were our only concern, it would be beyond our power to create. And there are other concerns which may stand in the way of the egalitarian ideal, such as the danger to liberty in the attempt to achieve it, as was Tocqueville's warning, the economic cost which might result, as was Arthur Okun's warning, or the avoidance of the kind of blandness in society which is a remembrance of what used to be East Berlin.

Not only is the idea of perfection illusive, it is also wrong and terribly, terribly dangerous. Imperfection is not a temporary inconvenience on the road to the promised land; it is a normal and permanent feature of all things people do. Visions of perfection make today insignificant because what we do now matters only to the degree that it advances the ultimate goal. Under such theories, democracy is unnecessary and science has no chance. From the experience of the collapse of communism it must be possible to say with authority, and from the experience of the rise of religious fundamentalism it must be right to say with emphasis, that the quest for perfection in human affairs is destructive of civilization and of dignity. This deserves to be repeated on every possible occasion in a time when it is accepted, even in this country, that a man should be condemned to death for some disrespectful remarks about religion. 'My dogma', writes Anthony Storr, 'is that all dogma is suspect.'

Rather than trying to turn democracy into dogma, we should seek practical, reasonable, working democracy. I have suggested that success in this depends much on citizens. We must want democracy and we must behave democratically. We need democratic laws and democratic institutions but these are only a framework. It is then for the citizens to take this framework and breathe life into it, or destroy it, by the way they use it.

There are theories, according to which the pursuit of self-interest on the part of individuals adds up to good society. I do not know if there are practical circumstances in which this works—I suspect not, it is too good to be true. Democracy is certainly not this kind of system. If citizens were to approach democracy in the what's-in-it-for-me spirit, it would collapse outright. There would be no reason to vote since each vote matters next to nothing; there would be no reason for those in advantage not to manipulate the policy process; there would be no reason for compliance. There would not even be a semblance of collective will, since, as Kenneth Arrow has shown, individual preferences do not add up to a single collective choice. No institutions can make voting a good investment of time, and no institutions can eliminate the element of sacrifice in compliance.

Well-organized society depends on rules and the policing of rules, but the role of rules is ambiguous. In a dictatorship, rules are a part of the repressive apparatus. In an open society, rules should reflect more than impose agreement and have as their main function to prevent disruptive free-riding problems on the fringes. In democracy, where the whole idea is that citizens regulate themselves, the role of rules must be limited. Some countries have made voting compulsory but this will do no good if people do not want to vote. Rules about compliance are necessary but there would not be much left in the democratic ideal if there were no more compliance than was enforced.

In a nutshell the problem is this: democracy assumes equality.

Equality we shall never have. Reasonable, working democracy therefore depends on the full force of inequality not being brought to bear on the democratic process. This cannot be done with rules alone; it would not work and would anyway be self-defeating. It must in great measure be done through voluntary restraint on self-interest. We must have integrity in political leadership; we must expect those in wealth to refrain from using the power of their wealth as a political tool; we must agree not to organize for political blackmail; we must request editors to allow free representation of opinion; we must ask pop stars and professors for modesty in being opinionated.

Am I then saying that democratic man cannot be rational man? I am not. Rational man wants liberty. Democracy protects liberty. Nothing could be more rational than to act in support of democracy. What I am rather saying is that rational man need not be egoistic man. Thoughtful action on the part of free persons cannot mean only the effective use of means for short-term satisfaction, it must also include the choice of goals. It is not beyond the wit of those who are concerned with the consequences of what they do, to grasp that the effectiveness of their own actions depends on how they interact with the actions of others, and the co-ordination of action is not the mystery it is sometimes made out to be once we allow for experience.

'In every scientific venture,' wrote Joseph Schumpeter in *History of Economic Analysis*, 'the thing that comes first is Vision.' Is there an Oxford vision for the social sciences? There are no doubt many, but it must be right to mention that of *justice*. The relevant works in moral philosophy, jurisprudence, economics, and sociology are too many to list; let me mention only Violet Butler's *Social Conditions in Oxford*, which is perhaps not among the most famous or glamorous of Oxford books but which was of importance for future activity in the University. It was published in 1912 and was an early case of empirical social research. In 1914 Barnett House was established to 'the advancement of economic and social studies'. Violet Butler became its Director of Studies in 1919. The House was subsequently made a University Department, and from its premises we today do research and offer training in social theory, social policy, and social work. In recent years, under the stimulating leadership of my predecessor, Professor A. H. Halsey, Oxford· has become firmly established at the forefront of the drive to make sociology scientific, without relinquishing relevance, through studies of education, stratification, and social trends.

In what sense is justice a vision? It is first of all a normative vision, something we believe in as a good thing. On this occasion, however, I have wanted to point out that justice is also an instrumental vision. If we take democracy as the value we are ultimately concerned with, the call for justice—or equality—is no longer only a statement of opinion, it is also an analytic result, reasonable equality being among the preconditions of practical democracy.

I would not want to say that democracy is dependent on the social sciences; of course not. However, I do not think it is immodest to suggest that high-quality social research inspired by the vision of justice can give support to democracy by contributing to satisfying, in Claus Moser's words, our need for an informed society.

On the side of strategy, I have suggested that the social scientist who wants to render service to democracy, should, as should the citizen participating in democracy, seek a balance between assertiveness and restraint. In this day and time of the me-generation, and of ideology crowding out pragmatism in government, and bearing in mind the over-opinionated nature of much that is said and written in my own field of research, that of social policy, I want to underline restraint. Neither in politics, nor in science—no more than in love, family, or friendship—can we succeed for ourselves or be of use for others if we always insist on holding our ground.

Here my story ends. Does democracy work? My remarks have been eminently old-fashioned ones. I have spoken of people rather than of structures. I have suggested that we as scientists have responsibility in our society. I have argued that democracy depends on democratically minded citizens and that we should apply restraint if we want to do good.

REFERENCES

ANDVIG, J. C., *Ragnar Frisch and the Great Depression* (Oslo, 1986).

ARROW, K., *Social Choice and Individual Values* (New York, 1963).

BOUDON, R., *La place du désordre* (Paris, 1984).

BUTLER, C. V., *Social Conditions in Oxford* (London, 1912).

DAHL, R. A., *A Preface to Economic Democracy* (Cambridge, 1985).

—— *Democracy and its Critics* (New Haven, 1989).

DAHRENDORF, R., *The Modern Social Conflict* (London, 1988).

—— *Reflections on the Revolution in Europe* (London, 1990).

FRISCH, R., *Innledning til produksjonsteorien* (Oslo, 1962).

GERTH, H. H., and WRIGHT MILLS, C., *From Max Weber: Essays in Sociology* (New York, 1946).

HALSEY, A. H., *Traditions of Social Policy: Essays in Honour of Violet Butler* (Oxford, 1976).

JOHANSSON, S., *Mot en teori för social rapportering* (Stockholm, 1977).

MOSER, C., *Our Need for an Informed Society*, Presidential Address to the British Association for the Advancement of Science (1990).

MYRDAL, G., *The Political Element in the Development of Economic Theory* (London, 1953).

OKUN, A. M., *Equality and Efficiency: The Big Trade-Off* (Washington DC, 1975).

PRZEWORSKI, A., *Democracy and the Market* (Cambridge, 1991).

RAWLS, J., *A Theory of Justice* (Cambridge, 1971).

RINGEN, S., *The Possibility of Politics* (Oxford, 1987).

ROBBINS, L. *An Essay on the Nature and Significance of Economic Science* (London, 1935).

SARTORI, G. *The Theory of Democracy Revisited, I–II* (Chatham, 1987).

SCHUMPETER, J., *A History of Economic Analysis* (Oxford and New York, 1954).

STORR, A., *Human Destructiveness* (New York, 1991).

TAWNEY, R. H., *Equality* (London, 1931).

TOCQUEVILLE, A., *De la démocratie en Amerique* (Paris, 1835–40).

ISBN 0 19 951359 7